ENCHANTED

Therapy Coloring Book

KAILEAH NELSON

KAILEAH NELSON

ISBN: 1548305138
ISBN-13: 978-1548305130

KAILEAH NELSON

Foggy Night Flight

KAILEAH NELSON

King of the Flowers

King of the Flowers

KAILEAH NELSON

Dragon's Valley

Rise of the Mushrooms

Tree Life

Lily of the Valley

Remnant

Lady of the Mire

Flying Ribbit

KAILEAH NELSON

Princess in the Clouds

KAILEAH NELSON

The Dragon Guardian

Dewdrop Mistress

KAILEAH NELSON

A Day with Father

The Peanut Butter Goblin

Misfit Mechanic

Teacup Mishap

The Cookie Fairy

White Wing

KAILEAH NELSON

Lady of the Falls

You and Me

Candy Fairy

Crash site

Silver Shire

KAILEAH NELSON

The Opossum Keeper

The Opossum Keeper

Hot Shot

Earth Whisperer

KAILEAH NELSON

Hop and Fly

The Pirate Brownie

Twin Sisters

KAILEAH NELSON

Winter Dance

Don't stop now. You're a color expert!
Amazon.com/author/kaileahnelson

Coming Soon...

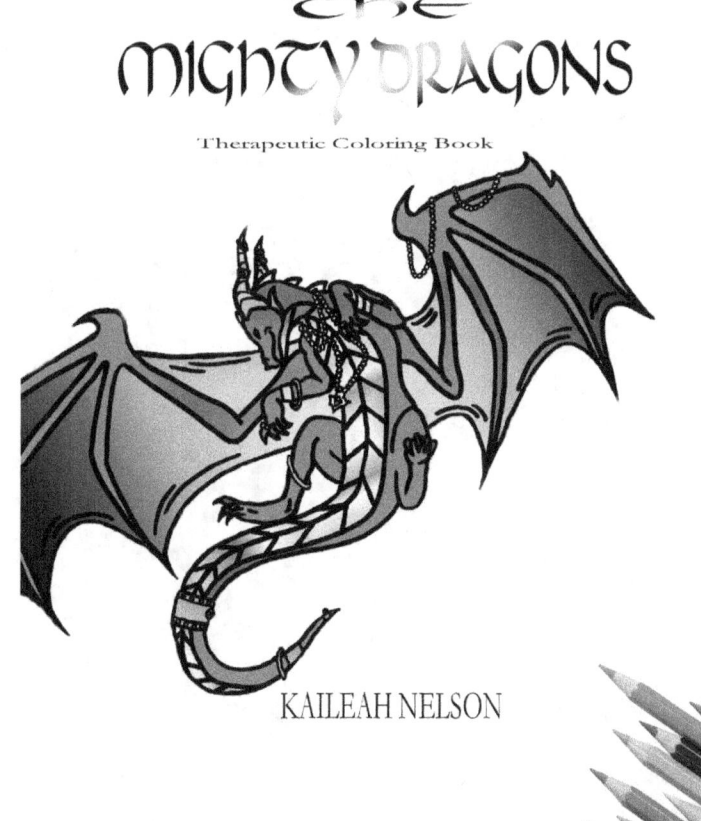

THE
MIGHTY DRAGONS

Therapeutic Coloring Book

KAILEAH NELSON